A CARTOON HISTORY
OF THE REAGAN YEARS

A Cartoon History of the REAGAN YEARS

Edited by
FRED BARNES
and featuring the cartoons of
Gary Brookins, Ed Gamble, Bob Gorrell,
Steve Kelley, Mike Luckovich,
Mike Peters, Ed Stein, and John Trever

REGNERY GATEWAY

Washington, D.C.

Library of Congress Cataloging-in-Publication Data

A Cartoon history of the Reagan years.

    1. United States—Politics and government—
1981–   —Caricatures and cartoons. 2. Reagan,
Ronald—Caricatures and cartoons. 3. American wit and
humor, Pictorial. I. Barnes, Fred, 1943–
E876.C38 1988   973.927'0207   88–4419
ISBN 0–89526–778–0

Published in the United States by
Regnery Gateway
1130 17th Street, NW
Washington, DC 20036

Distributed to the trade by
Kampmann & Company, Inc.
9 E 40th Street
New York, NY 10016

10 9 8 7 6 5 4 3 2 1

Contents

1980

THE RISE OF REAGAN

Democrats relished the idea of facing Ronald Reagan as the Republican presidential nominee. They figured he'd be easy to tag as a right-wing extremist, an aging ex-actor, and a dope. They figured wrong. Reagan committed gaffes and goofs, but his appeal was magnetic. He attracted Southern and ethnic Democrats, independents, yuppies, and, of course, conservatives and Republicans. The Age of the Gipper had arrived.

Warmonger   Would this genial fellow start World War III? Nope, said voters.

Race   Carter said Reagan would pit whites against blacks.
This charge didn't make Reagan's view on race a big issue, but it
did shed light on Carter's meanness.

Age   "The O & W" was Reagan's nickname, the Oldest and Wisest. He was 69, but didn't seem a day older than 68. Well, maybe 68-and-a-half.

Actor   Only in America could an actor of modest success run for president, tell scores of Hollywood stories during the campaign, and still win the White House.

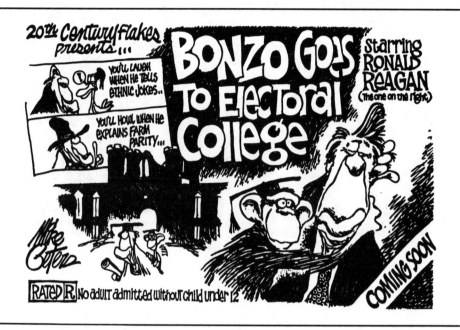

"CAN YOU BELIEVE IT? A LOUSY, STINKIN' <u>ACTOR</u> IN THE WHITE HOUSE!"

"He's the one in the suit, comrade!"

NEWS ITEM: SCIENTISTS HAVE FOUND WHAT IS BELIEVED TO BE THE OLDEST FOSSIL FOOTPRINTS

THE RISE OF REAGAN

Mainstream   Reagan's not in it, Democrats insisted. It's Democrats who aren't, the voters replied.

"THE DANGER WITH REAGAN IS, HE'S NOT IN THE MAINSTREAM!"

Kooky   Aren't some of Reagan's views a bit strange? Oh, there you go again.

"HE'S COMING IN... HE'S COMING IN... IT'S EVERY MAN FOR HIMSELF!"

THE RISE OF REAGAN

Women   The 1970s made Reagan more conservative than ever on one issue, the Equal Rights Amendment. Against the ERA, for women's rights—that's Reagan.

"WANT SOME MORE PEANUTS, DEAR?"

Carter   The public recoiled at the idea of four more years of Jimmy Carter, and Rosalyn, and Amy, and Billy, and. . . . Spare us more mush from the wimp.

"You're gonna love this, Ron... it's the Rose Garden! It's where I spend most of my time working!"

...everything I said about Carter.... incompetent, Hoover's clone, a laughing stock... a pure disaster.... well I was just kidding..!

Bedfellows   Carter fiddled while the Ayatollah fumed and kept Americans hostage for 444 days. And Reagan won.

THE RISE OF REAGAN

1981
THE LEGEND BEGINS

Reagan had scarcely gotten to Washington when he took a hit—a would-be assassin's bullet—and came up quipping. "Honey, I forgot to duck," he told Nancy. Clearly this was no wimp. As if to prove the point, he fired striking air traffic controllers, all of them. Oh, yes, the Gipper slashed federal spending and won enactment of a deep tax cut. From day one, it was Reagan's year.

Shooting John Hinckley had no trouble getting a gun. Slowing up Reagan was something else again.

"AMERICA! THE LAND OF OPPORTUNITY— WHERE ANYBODY CAN SET HIS SIGHTS ON THE HIGHEST OFFICE IN THE NATION!"

TRUE GRIT!

Strike A lesson air traffic controllers learned the hard way: Don't dare Reagan to fire you. You'll only make his day.

"IT SAYS HERE..."HANG TOUGH AND YOU'LL HAVE THEM IN THE PALMS OF YOUR HANDS."

"AT LEAST WE SUCCEEDED IN FORCING REAGAN TO GIVE US ONE OF
OUR DEMANDS— A SHORTER WORK WEEK."

THE LEGEND BEGINS

Budget　　For decades, Reagan spoke on the chicken-dinner circuit about cutting federal spending. When he had a chance, he jumped at it.

"EXCUSE ME, MR. STOCKMAN, BUT ONE OF THE NAVIGATORS WHO STEERED US INTO THIS WISHES TO PROTEST YOUR CRUEL AND INHUMANE METHODS...."

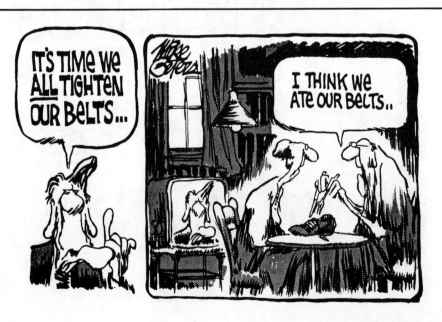

IT'S TIME WE ALL TIGHTEN OUR BELTS...

I THINK WE ATE OUR BELTS..

THE LEGEND BEGINS

HE SAID 'ABSOLUTELY NO HANDOUTS'... BUT, HE'D HELP US
APPLY FOR A SMALL BUSINESS LOAN...

I DON'T CARE IF HE IS YOUR BUDGET DIRECTOR... HE'S GIVING ME THE WILLIES...

CUTTING ROOM

THE BUDGET

THE LEGEND BEGINS

THE LEGEND BEGINS

THE LEGEND BEGINS

Supply-side   Reagan's enormous cut in tax rates will cause more inflation and/or a recession, his foes said. No way. It touched off sustained economic growth without high inflation.

THE LEGEND BEGINS

Fallback   Stunned by Reagan's success, critics came up with a new argument. He doesn't know where he's going.

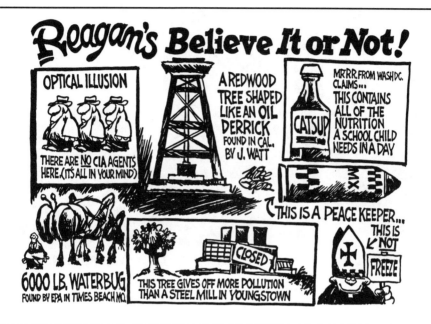

AMERICAN FOLKLORE: RONALD REAGAN THROWS 222 BILLION DOLLARS ACROSS THE POTOMAC.

"THIS ROAD IS NOT ON THE MAP,... BUT IT'S GOTTA BE BETTER THAN THE ONE WE'VE BEEN ON!"

"REMEMBER, A JOURNEY OF A THOUSAND MILES BEGINS WITH A SINGLE STEP!"

THE LEGEND BEGINS

Detached When a crisis arrives, Reagan is forced to spend sleepless afternoons in the Oval Office. Reagan was told hard work isn't fatal, but why take a chance?

Academy   Pity the poor political science professors put out of work by a successful, popular president. Their courses in The Troubled Presidency and The Decline of the White House don't fly anymore.

"HE JUST COMPLETED THE DEFINITIVE, 600-PAGE WORK ON WHY SPECIAL-INTEREST GROUPS, WEAK PARTIES AND A FRAGMENTED CONGRESS MAKE PRESIDENTIAL LEADERSHIP IMPOSSIBLE."

1982
THE LEGEND SOURS

When times turn bad on your watch, you get the blame. And Reagan did. The recession was the deepest since the Depression. Reagan seemed confused. He raised taxes. His military buildup drew barbs. His relations with both European allies and Soviet foes were chilly. And as luck would have it, there was trouble at home: the First Lady. As joblessness grew, she bought expensive new china. At year's end, the worst came, a congressional election in which Reagan's GOP was humiliated.

Downturn   Okay, okay, Reagan's tax cut hadn't gone into effect yet. But the budget cuts have—pain without prosperity.

THE LEGEND SOURS

HE SAYS THERE'S NO ROOM... BUT IF WE'RE TRULY NEEDY,
WE CAN TRY THE STABLE IN THE PRIVATE SECTOR.

THE LEGEND SOURS

"HEY! I CAN FEEL IT — WE'RE TURNING AROUND!"

THE LEGEND SOURS

Reaganomics   This is Monday, so we must be cutting taxes. Or are we raising taxes? Well, it's one or the other.

HIS FANTASY, TATTOO?... HE WANTS TO CUT TAXES, INCREASE DEFENSES AND BALANCE THE BUDGET ALL AT THE SAME TIME...

THE LEGEND SOURS

"...AND THIS IS OUR WORKING MODEL...."

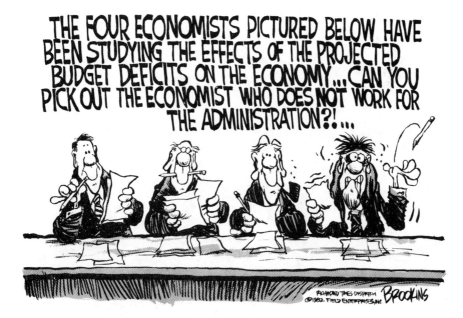

"SO THIS IS THE **REAGAN REVOLUTION** WE'VE HEARD SO MUCH ABOUT...."

"HEY, KEMP!... THAT LOOKS LIKE SOME OF <u>OUR</u> GUYS OUT THERE!"

THE LEGEND SOURS

Defense   Building up the nation's military capability was one of Reagan's greatest achievements. But few thought so during the recession year.

"FOOLS! THEY DO NOT UNDERSTAND! THEY ARE MISLED... MANIPULATED BY OUR ENEMIES!"

THE LEGEND SOURS

"STOP COMPLAINING AND SWALLOW— THIS IS FOR YOUR OWN GOOD!"

50   THE LEGEND SOURS

Ideas   Everybody loves a new idea, right? Not if it costs them money from Washington.

"LET YOU FILL THE BUCKET? HOW DID REAGAN COME UP WITH A FAR-FETCHED IDEA LIKE THAT?!"

"TRUST ME TONTO... IN A COUPLE OF YEARS FROM NOW YOU'LL BE THANKING ME!"

THE LEGEND SOURS

Lifestyle   Reagan made the job look so simple. Of course he wasn't around some of the time, and Nancy had her shortcomings.

"HONEST, AL... THEY'RE JUST DOODLES!... I'M NOT TAKING NOTES ON YOU IN CODE TO LEAK TO THE PRESS!"

THE LEGEND SOURS

Chill   Reagan was willing to deny the Soviets anything, including a gas pipeline to Europe. Anything, that is, but grain for sale from U.S. farmers.

"IF YOU CAN'T STAND THE COLD, GET OUT OF THE FREEZER...."

"THE LAST THING I REMEMBER IS LIGHTING THIS CANDLE FOR POLAND...."

'Oops! I misread that . . . It says he's concerned about the POLLS.

THE LEGEND SOURS

THE LEGEND SOURS

Containment   This policy had its day with Reagan. The Communist advance had to be stopped somewhere, which turned out to be El Salvador.

THE LEGEND SOURS

Deficit   Attacks on Democratic deficits were a staple of Reagan speeches. The recession and his failure to win new spending cuts gave him his own deficit to worry about.

"I HAVE A FUNNY FEELING HOW ALL THIS IS GOING TO END...."

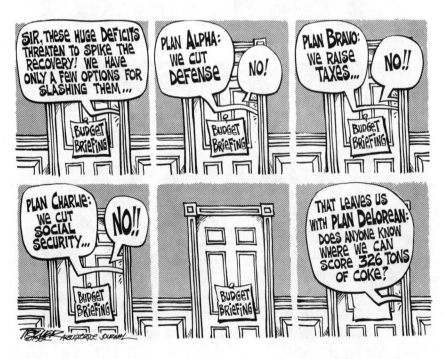

THE LEGEND SOURS

"WOULD YOU BOYS KINDLY EXCUSE ME A MOMENT? I GOTTA GO PREACH...."

THE LEGEND SOURS

Election   The worst of all political worlds is being the party in power during a recession. Republicans were. Reagan said things would soon be better, and they were. But not by November, when Republicans lost 26 House seats.

WHAT IS THE WORST PROBLEM JIMMY CARTER LEFT US WITH?

JOBS

UNEMPLOYMENT   INFLATION

THIS IS A TEST... THIS IS ONLY A TEST... IF THIS HAD BEEN AN ACTUAL PRESIDENTIAL ELECTION, YOU WOULD HAVE BEEN ANNIHILATED...

"AH, YES — IT'S THE PARTY THAT MADE REAGANOMICS POSSIBLE...."

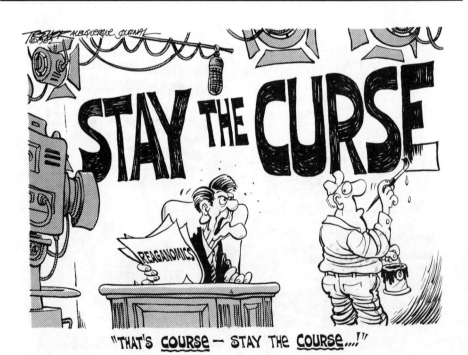

"THAT'S _COURSE_ — STAY THE _COURSE_....!"

THE LEGEND SOURS

1983
★★★★THE LEGEND REVIVES

Reagan came into the year like Jimmy Carter and came out like FDR. And the notion that, above all, Reagan is lucky took hold. It's nonsense, but one thing is certain: The guy ain't *un*lucky. Reagan's nuke-the-whales viewpoint on the environment got him in hot water, as did the deployment of troops to Lebanon. But then came the invasion of Grenada, a success for freedom. But the best news was the economy. It boomed. When that happens on your watch, you get the credit.

Lebanon   Reagan's knowledge of the Middle East is minimal, and thus he's persuadable. He took bad advice in sending Marines to Lebanon, where 256 were killed.

THE LEGEND REVIVES

Pollution   If the scandal at the Environmental Protection
Administration wasn't enough, Reagan had Interior Secretary
James Watt to deal with. His solution was to fire everybody.

THE LEGEND REVIVES

IT'S RAINING..IT'S POURING..THE OLD MAN IS SNORING..

Russkies   Reagan's strategy was to convince them he was interested in an arms buildup, not arms control, all so they'd make concessions. His act was so convincing you'd almost have thought he wasn't acting.

THE LEGEND REVIVES

THE LEGEND REVIVES

THE LEGEND REVIVES

Neighbors   Intervention in Central America was no crowd-pleaser, but freeing American students in Grenada—and the citizens of Grenada—brought the house down. Bravo!

THE LEGEND REVIVES

"C'MON! YOU GOTTA JUMP RIGHT BACK IN, OR YOU'LL <u>NEVER</u> GET OVER IT!"

"I'M MAD AS HELL ...AND I'M NOT GOING TO TAKE IT ANYMORE !!!"

THE LEGEND REVIVES

THE LEGEND REVIVES

THE LEGEND REVIVES

"QUICK! MORE QUARTERS!"

THE LEGEND REVIVES

81

"GOOD GRIEF!... THIS LOOKS LIKE ANOTHER *VIETNAM*...!"

Training   With a re-election race in sight, Reagan had to start
wooing angry minorities—women, blacks, Hispanics, the press.

"IS IT MY IMAGINATION OR ARE THESE PRESS CONFERENCES GETTING TOUGHER?"

THE LEGEND REVIVES

THE LEGEND REVIVES

THE LEGEND REVIVES

Roar   Treasury Secretary Donald Regan promised the economy would come "roaring back." He was right.

"WELL, REAGAN'S MANAGED TO GET THE COUNTRY MOVING AGAIN....."

"EVERYBODY OUT....I THINK IT'S OVER!"

THE LEGEND REVIVES

THE LEGEND REVIVES

1984
THE LEGEND TRIUMPHS

Get this. A 73-year-old guy who can't hear too well and gives lots of folks the willies is running for re-election. He wins easily. This is not a paradox. Reagan tidied up his troubles. He was no longer as aloof about negotiating with the Soviets and no longer as chummy toward the Religious Right. Best of all, he had an economic upturn and a poor but honorable opponent, Walter Mondale, on his hands. Once Mondale vowed to raise taxes, Reagan had him right where he wanted him.

Tête-à-tête   Two months before election day, Reagan invited Soviet Foreign Minister Andrei Gromyko to the White House for a chat. It was a great photo opportunity.

THE LEGEND TRIUMPHS

THE LEGEND TRIUMPHS

Cap   Though Defense Secretary Caspar Weinberger, a Reagan
favorite, squawked, the Pentagon got its budget trimmed.
Another crowd pleaser.

Majority Aides warned Reagan to keep away from the Christian Right, but Reagan wanted to make them part of his personal moral majority.

THE LEGEND TRIUMPHS

Flag Reagan not only wrapped himself in the American flag, an old politician's trick, but he also identified himself with the Olympics and D-day. Good show.

"WOULD YOU LIKE TO RESPOND TO THAT, MR. MONDALE? AND, PLEASE, DON'T WHINE!"

THE LEGEND TRIUMPHS

"YOU ARE FEELING GOOD...YOU ARE BETTER OFF... YOU ARE GETTING SLEEPY...."

THE LEGEND TRIUMPHS

"THEN AGAIN, I SUPPOSE HE DOESN'T REALLY NEED A PLATFORM...."

"HEY, EDNA — THE REAGAN INTRODUCTION FILM IS ON...."

THE LEGEND TRIUMPHS

THE LEGEND TRIUMPHS

Taxes Mondale said he'd raise 'em. Reagan said he wouldn't. The voters said Reagan's the one.

THE LEGEND TRIUMPHS

THE LEGEND TRIUMPHS

Deficit   Mondale talked about it a lot. Reagan pretended Mondale was talking about some imaginary rabbit. The deficit became Mondale's Harvey.

THE LEGEND TRIUMPHS

"OK, GUYS, INTO THE FREEZER, QUICK — BEFORE IT STARTS TO SMELL...."

THE LEGEND TRIUMPHS

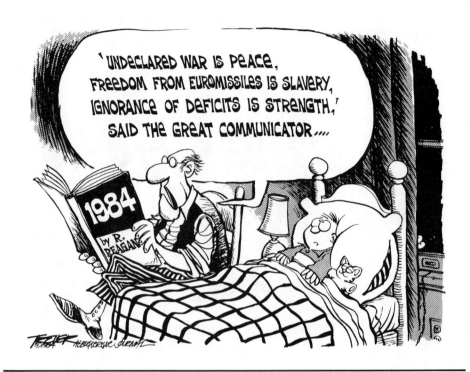

THE LEGEND TRIUMPHS

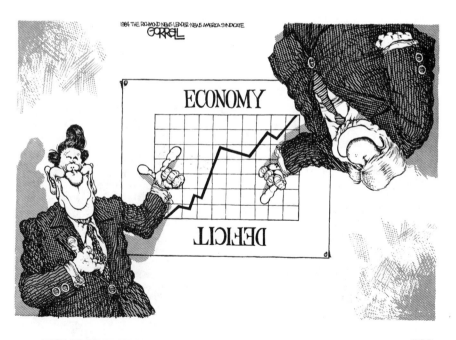

THE LEGEND TRIUMPHS

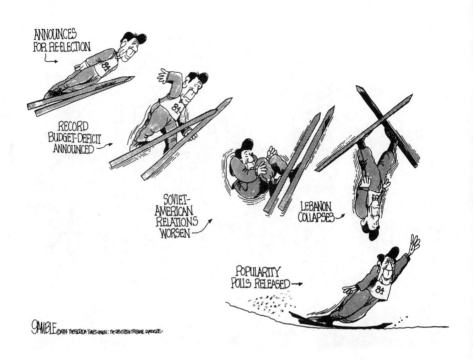

ANNOUNCES FOR RE-ELECTION

RECORD BUDGET-DEFICIT ANNOUNCED

SOVIET-AMERICAN RELATIONS WORSEN

LEBANON COLLAPSES

POPULARITY POLLS RELEASED

"WELL, THERE GOES MARTIN FELDSTEIN... GEE, THAT'S TOO BAD!-- HE WAS THE ADMINISTRATION'S LAST LINK TO ECONOMIC REALITY!!......"

THE LEGEND TRIUMPHS

Age   Reagan looked ancient in debate with Mondale, then said he wouldn't let the age issue intrude in the race. Mondale's youth and inexperience—these he'd ignore. Voters laughed, and ignored the Gipper's age.

THE LEGEND TRIUMPHS

THE LEGEND TRIUMPHS

Forty-niner Try as he might—and he added an extra campaign stop in Minnesota—Reagan was unable to win 50 states. Minnesota eluded him.

"THIS SHOULD BE EASY PICKINGS.... I HEAR REAGAN'S ALREADY A LAME DUCK...!"

"THAT'S WHAT I SAID, CHIEF... MR. MONDALE TRIED TO BRING ALL HIS SPECIAL INTEREST GROUPS ACROSS THE BRIDGE AT THE SAME TIME!!"

THE LEGEND TRIUMPHS

THE DAY AFTER

"WE SEEM TO HAVE A QUORUM — MAYBE THIS IS A GOOD TIME TO DISCUSS THAT CHANGE IN DIRECTION...."

THE LEGEND TRIUMPHS

1985
THE LEGEND OVERREACHES

More popular than Dwight Eisenhower. More decorated with accomplishments than Franklin Roosevelt. More dominant in Washington than Lyndon Johnson. That was Reagan. At 73, he was the oldest president in history, at the start of his second term. But when things are going your way inside the Beltway, beware. Trouble always lurks. The Reagan agenda was running dry. Only tax reform was left. What would fill the agenda gap? Heaven only knew.

Teflon   Nothing could bring down SuperReagan, not even the press. Or so it seemed.

THE LEGEND OVERREACHES

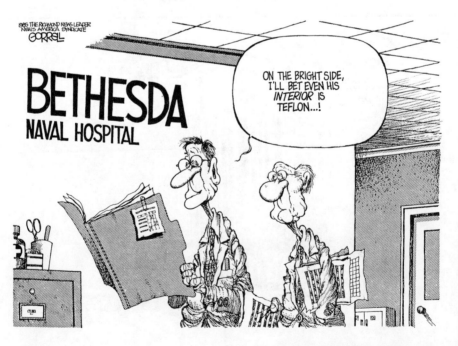

THE LEGEND OVERREACHES

Taxes   Reagan didn't give a hoot about eliminating tax loopholes, but he wanted to get individual tax rates down more. A tax reform bill was the vehicle.

THE OLD MAN AND THE SEA OF SPECIAL INTERESTS

THE LEGEND OVERREACHES

       THE LEGEND OVERREACHES

Terrorists Reagan talked tough, but when TWA 847 was hijacked, he carried a wet noodle. He saved the big stick for Muammar Gaddafi.

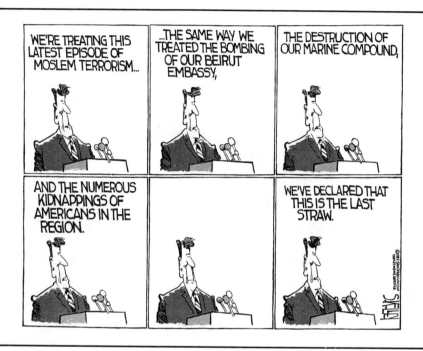

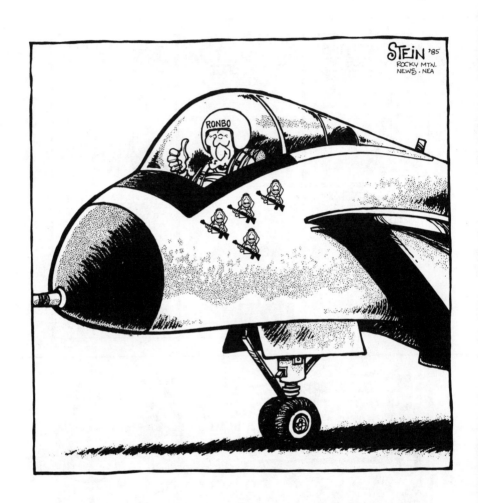

THE LEGEND OVERREACHES

THE LEGEND OVERREACHES
127

"WELL, WELL, WELL... LOOK WHAT THE TOMCAT DRAGGED IN!"

THE LEGEND OVERREACHES

"FIRST OF ALL....YOU GUYS ARE IN REALLY BIG TROUBLE !!"

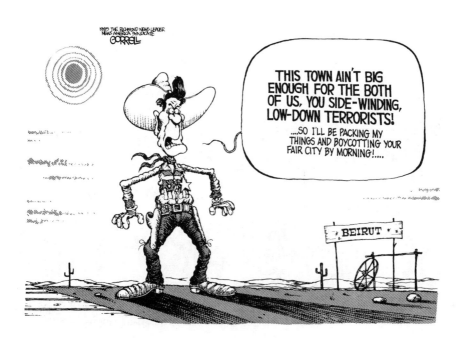

THE LEGEND OVERREACHES

Contras   Getting Congress to fund the contras in Nicaragua was never a cinch. Reagan was unrelenting, though.

THE LEGEND OVERREACHES

"DELIBERATELY UNDERESTIMATING ENEMY STRENGTH, HM? WELL, WE WON'T LET *THAT* HAPPEN AGAIN...."

THE LEGEND OVERREACHES

THE LEGEND OVERREACHES

Apartheid   Protests against South Africa's racial policy made Reagan's stance of "constructive engagement" a big item on the national agenda.

THE LEGEND OVERREACHES

Bitburg It seemed harmless enough, a speech honoring the German war dead. When Reagan found out some of the dead were Nazis, he went to Bitburg cemetery anyway.

THE LEGEND OVERREACHES

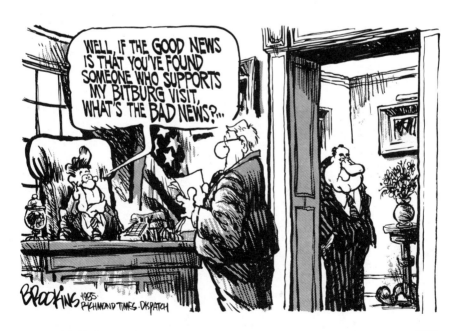

THE LEGEND OVERREACHES

Promise   Reagan had vowed to balance the budget by 1984.
He wasn't off by much, only about $180 billion.

THE LEGEND OVERREACHES

THE LEGEND OVERREACHES

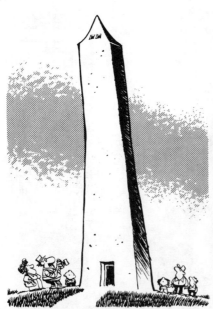

WASHINGTON MONUMENT

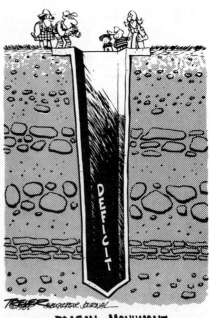

REAGAN MONUMENT

THE LEGEND OVERREACHES

THE LEGEND OVERREACHES

Summit   For the first time, Reagan met with a Soviet leader. Everybody thought Mikhail Gorbachev would overwhelm him. But Gorbo was overwhelmed.

"TRUST ME — IT'S THE FASTEST WAY TO GENEVA!"

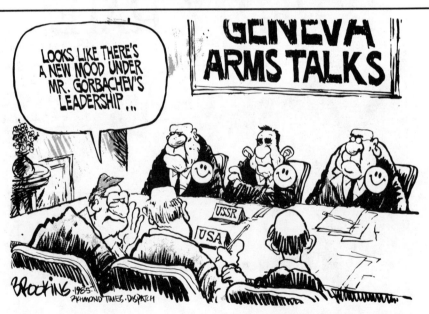

THE LEGEND OVERREACHES

THE LEGEND OVERREACHES

REAGAN'S CHANGED HIS MIND AGAIN...NOW HE JUST WANTS TO HAVE A TUPPERWARE PARTY.

THE LEGEND OVERREACHES

THE LEGEND OVERREACHES

THE LEGEND OVERREACHES

THE LEGEND OVERREACHES

1986
THE LEGEND STUMBLES

In early November, Reagan's rating reached 69 percent—better than two-thirds of the people thought he was doing a good job. That was amazingly high for a second-term president. It didn't last long. By late autumn, the Iran-contra affair had been revealed, the Senate had gone Democratic, and 20 points had been shaved off Reagan's popularity. He joked: "Remember when I said we'd bomb Russia in five minutes? Remember when I dozed off on the Pope? Remember Bitburg? Those were the good old days."

Verdict   The preliminary judgment was a failed second term. The press said Reagan was too old, too caught up in scandal, too detached.

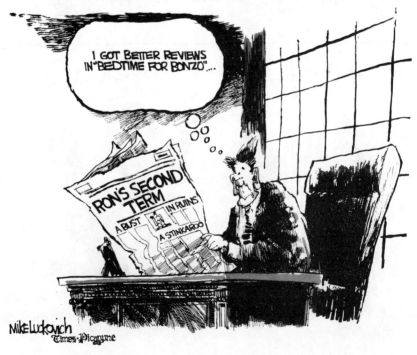

THE LEGEND STUMBLES

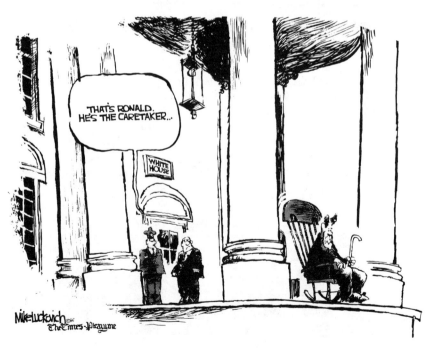

THE LEGEND STUMBLES

THE LEGEND STUMBLES

"NOT ONLY THAT. ALL THE TEFLON SEEMS TO HAVE WASHED OFF...."

THE LEGEND STUMBLES

Iranamok   Reagan could have done just about anything and still been beloved. Anything but sell arms to the Ayatollah.

THE LEGEND STUMBLES

THE LEGEND STUMBLES

THE LEGEND STUMBLES

"THE TIME HAS COME, MR. PRESIDENT, TO CONSIDER CREATING THE 'DEPARTMENT OF HOSTAGES, SPIES, AND SWAPS'....."

THE LEGEND STUMBLES

THE LEGEND STUMBLES

Shortfall   If there was a respite from worrying about
Iranamok, there was always the budget to fret over.

THE LEGEND STUMBLES

"NOTHING—JUST RED INK...."

THE LEGEND STUMBLES

"NOW THAT'S GOING TOO FAR!!"

BETTER GET SOMEBODY OVER HERE...HE WANTS TO
ORGANIZE A DEFICIT AID CONCERT...

THE LEGEND STUMBLES

Good The allies in Europe, except England's magnificent Maggie Thatcher, wouldn't go along, but the raid on Libya was a great success. Terrorist acts declined.

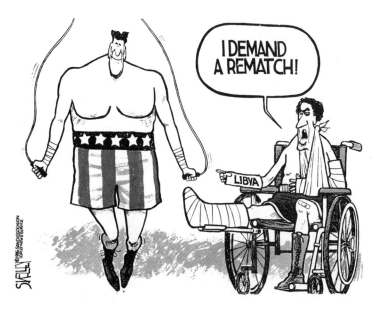

THE LEGEND STUMBLES

GETTING HIS
EUROPEAN
DUCKS IN A ROW...

THE LEGEND STUMBLES

THE LEGEND STUMBLES

THE LEGEND STUMBLES

Bad   Bulging with overconfidence, Reagan rushed off to
Iceland for a second summit with Gorbo. This time, Reagan
flopped.

THE LEGEND STUMBLES   169

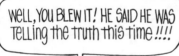

THE LEGEND STUMBLES

"WE'VE GOT TO STOP MEETING LIKE THIS...."

THE LEGEND STUMBLES

Better   Reagan and friends overpowered the special interests and got tax reform through. Imagine a top rate at 28 percent—no small feat.

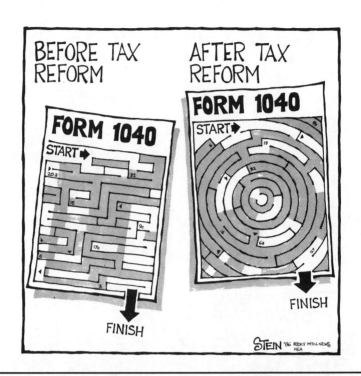

THE LEGEND STUMBLES

THE LEGEND STUMBLES

175

Worse   Despite Reagan's barnstorming for months, the Senate fell into Democratic hands. This was ominous.

THE LEGEND STUMBLES

THE LEGEND STUMBLES

Refrain   Reagan's song about those freedom fighters in Nicaragua was falling from the hit parade. Congress and the public were listening to peace music from Managua.

THE LEGEND STUMBLES

THE LEGEND STUMBLES   179

THE LEGEND STUMBLES

1987

THE LEGEND HITS BOTTOM

Iranamok sapped Reagan's time and his spirit.
When the New York Giants came for White House
congratulations after winning the National Football
League championship, the president said the cheering
was from their fans. "I don't have any fans anymore,"
he said sadly. Reagan took his lumps in the Iranamok
hearings on Capitol Hill. Then, his personal
choice for the Supreme Court, Robert Bork, was
defeated. Reagan seemed a lamer than usual duck.
But his spirits—and his popularity—soared when his
deployment of warships in the Persian Gulf worked
and the Washington summit with Gorbo was a TV
dazzler.

Befuddled   Iranamok confused Reagan. He said his overtures to Iran had unfortunately become arms-for-hostages, then said the opposite.

"SPECIAL EFFECTS?!! . . ."

THE LEGEND HITS BOTTOM

THE LEGEND HITS BOTTOM

THE LEGEND HITS BOTTOM

THE LEGEND HITS BOTTOM

Hearings   Ollie North made himself a hero in nationally televised testimony. But he didn't relieve his commander-in-chief's Iranamok gloom.

THE LEGEND HITS BOTTOM

FAMOUS PRESIDENTIAL QUOTATIONS:

THE LEGEND HITS BOTTOM

The Reagan Memoirs:

THE LEGEND HITS BOTTOM

191

THE LEGEND HITS BOTTOM

THE LEGEND HITS BOTTOM

THE LAST IRAN-CONTRA HEARINGS' WITNESS!

"HI, GUYS...WHAT ARE YOU...WHOOPS! NEVER MIND...IT'S PROBABLY SOMETHING I DON'T NEED TO KNOW!"

THE LEGEND HITS BOTTOM

WHAT'S COMING OUT OF THE IRAN-CONTRA HEARINGS!

Lynching Never before had liberals been so united against Reagan as they were when Bork was nominated.

THE LEGEND HITS BOTTOM

THE LEGEND HITS BOTTOM

Compromise   It would be a cold day in hell before Reagan agreed to accept a tax hike. That day came October 19, when the stock market crashed.

"EVERYTHING IS ON THE TABLE...."

THE LEGEND HITS BOTTOM

THE LEGEND HITS BOTTOM

Right   For two decades, Reagan's base was the conservative
movement. But even the best of friends grow distant.

THE LEGEND HITS BOTTOM

THE LEGEND HITS BOTTOM

Trade   The president was bedeviled by twin deficits, the second one on trade. It took all Reagan's might to forestall protectionism.

THE LEGEND HITS BOTTOM

"HORRIBLE!...EVERYTHING WAS FINE UNTIL I GOT TO THE WHITE HOUSE. THEN REAGAN ACCUSED ME OF DUMPING BELOW COST AND DEMANDED A 100% TARIFF....."

"HAW! CAN YOU BELIEVE THAT REAGAN?! HE ACTUALLY THINKS A SPACE SHIELD WILL PROTECT US FROM ATTACK!"

THE LEGEND HITS BOTTOM

THE LEGEND HITS BOTTOM

Gulf It looked awfully risky—American ships amid the mines in the Persian Gulf and Kuwaiti barges flying the Stars and Stripes. But the oil flowed.

THE LEGEND HITS BOTTOM

THE LEGEND HITS BOTTOM

THE LEGEND HITS BOTTOM

THE LEGEND HITS BOTTOM

Rescue   In Reagan's darkest hour, Gorbo rushed to Washington. Reagan talked, but bargained tough, exactly what the American people wanted.

THE LEGEND HITS BOTTOM

THE LEGEND HITS BOTTOM   211

THE LEGEND HITS BOTTOM

Afterword:
THE REAGAN LEGACY

A single question dominated Washington in Ronald Reagan's eight years. How does this guy do it, this fellow who former Defense Secretary Clark Clifford called "an amiable dunce" and *Newsweek* said was painfully "detached" from day-to-day decision-making? As luck would have it, Reagan had an answer. He told the story of the two psychiatrists in private practice together. When they showed up for work, both were immaculate, bright-eyed, and smiling. But after a day of seeing patients, the young psychiatrist was frowning and disheveled, with worry lines rippling across his forehead. The old guy, though, was as fresh and beaming as ever. After weeks of this, the youngster finally popped the question to the old guy: "How come you're still the same after a tough day." The old shrink paused, then said, "I never listen." Reagan always smiles at the punch line.

Despite it all, Reagan was a successful president. He ranks below the Founding Fathers and Lincoln and even Franklin Roosevelt (you don't have to like FDR to recognize that he largely succeeded in his aims). But Reagan accomplished more than Carter, Ford, Nixon, Kennedy, and Eisenhower. With Johnson, it's a close call. In Johnson's years, a large tax cut, Medicare, the Civil Rights Act, the Voting Rights Act, and the antipoverty program were enacted, and the war in Vietnam was pursued, usually in too tepid a fashion. In Reagan's, a large tax cut, tax reform, a treaty banning medium-range nuclear missiles, and Star Wars came to pass, and a war in Nicaragua was pursued, usually in too tepid a fashion.

There were two big ironies in Reagan's success. First, he came to the presidency with plans to slay the Washington dragon, to make Washington and the federal government smaller forces in American life. After eight years, they loom as big as ever. The feds spend more, not less, and

Washington now serves as a magnet for conservatives as well as liberals. They flock to the city, and rarely return home. A conservative infrastructure has grown up in Washington—lawyers, lobbyists, journalists, think tanks, issue groups, publishers, etc. Washington is a different town after Reagan. But smaller and less influential, it isn't. Second, Reagan succeeded swimmingly in exactly those foreign policy areas where he had no intention of doing much, namely arms control and human rights. Who'd have guessed? Reagan's approach to arms control was exactly what the Soviets feared, and responded to. On intermediate-range missiles, Reagan said, "Here's my offer. Take it or leave it." When the Soviets balked in the past, presidents sheepishly rushed out a new proposal, then another and another. Reagan didn't, and six years later the Soviets accepted his offer. In 1987, he and Mikhail Gorbachev signed the INF Treaty, in Washington and on Reagan's terms. On intercontinental missiles, Reagan had another tack. He opted for Star Wars, a system to swat incoming missiles out of the sky. The Soviets fumed, but soon were offering concession after concession. The Reagan strategy worked, and brought rich, new definition to the phrase "peace through strength."

Reagan thought Carter had erred badly in zinging American allies, even autocratic ones, for human rights violations. And he vowed not to repeat the error. He didn't. Instead, Reagan and his aides waited until the prospects for democracy ripened. Then they moved. In the Philippines, they eased Ferdinand Marcos out of power, averting bloodshed. In South Korea, they prodded the government to grant a presidential election. The most pro-American candidate won. In Haiti, they speeded Baby Doc's departure. In Central America, they planted the first roots of democracy in Honduras, Guatemala, and El Salvador. In short, they achieved an impressive record.

In some of Reagan's ventures, there was no irony at all. He invaded Grenada and ousted Communist oppressors. He bombed Libya and punished Gaddafi for sending terrorist squads around the world. He dispatched troops to Honduras and scared the Sandinistas away from their final offensive against the contras. Sadly, Reagan lost much of his moral credibility by selling arms to Iran. Was it arms-for-hostages? That hardly matters. It was arms for a bitter, evil foe of America, and it was wrong.

What Reagan did best was be Reagan. He changed the

political landscape. Because of Reagan, politicians and presidential candidates are wary of advocating tax increases. And few are arguing for more and bigger government. Everyone now says traditional values, a favorite Reagan talking point, should be preserved. True, some of this is lip service, but at least it is new lip service. On national security, the idea that a president should be assertive in promoting the national interest was revived. Apologizing for America's role in the world went out of style, thanks to Reagan.

As a national leader, Reagan had what so many—Ford, Carter, Nixon—lacked. He could move people. His speech from Normandy commemorating D-day was a true tear-jerker, a powerful expression of Reagan's own feelings about America. His speeches turned the nation toward spending cuts and a deep tax reduction in 1981. And so on, speech after speech. Just as important was his personal conduct. He was genial, tough, and kindly, unfailingly so. When he was shot by an assassin and later afflicted with cancer, he brushed aside the danger with a quip.

Reagan's foes were disarmed by his charm. He was, said Governor Mario Cuomo of New York, "a moral instruction to my children, and to me." Cuomo lauded the way Reagan "deported himself. He's always unflappable. He never appears to be mean or ugly toward other human beings. If he has a fault with his friends, he's too loyal. But if you measure his conduct, it is at all times gentle, affectionate, controlled, disciplined. He's not a brilliant articulator of religious dogma, but the way he handled the cancer, the way he handled the shooting, instructed us in perspective and adjusting to God's will and taking it with equanimity. He doesn't talk about these things. But his personal conduct— you cannot measure the importance of the silent homily he delivered. There's an explanation in there somewhere for the vote he gets in polls and would get in another election. He's beloved."

Reagan will be missed, and by cartoonists more than most.

A CARTOON HISTORY OF THE REAGAN YEARS